P9-BYH-430

This book

Written and compiled by
Christina Goodings
Illustrations copyright © 2012
Emily Bolam
This edition copyright © 2012
Lion Hudson

The moral rights of the author
and illustrator have been asserted

A Lion Children's Book
an imprint of
Lion Hudson plc
Wilkinson House,
Jordan Hill Road,
Oxford OX2 8DR, England
www.lionhudson.com
ISBN 978 0 7459 6346 4 (print)
ISBN 978 0 7459 6736 3 (epub)
ISBN 978 0 7459 6737 0 (PDF)

First edition 2012
10 9 8 7 6 5 4 3 2 1 0
First electronic edition 2012

Acknowledgments
All unattributed prayers are by
Christina Goodings and Lois
Rock, copyright © Lion Hudson.
Prayers by Sophie Piper and
Victoria Tebbs are copyright ©
Lion Hudson.

Bible extracts are adapted from
the Good News Bible published
by the Bible Societies and
HarperCollins Publishers, ©
American Bible Society 1994,
used with permission.
The Lord's Prayer as it appears
in *Common Worship: Services and
Prayers for the Church of England*
(Church House Publishing,
2000) is copyright © The English
Language Liturgical Consultation
and is reproduced by permission
of the publisher.
Prayer by Blessed Teresa of
Calcutta used by permission.

A catalogue record for this book is
available from the British Library

Typeset in 14/17 Goudy Old Style
Printed in China August 2012
(manufacturer LH17)

Distributed by:
UK: Marston Book Services Ltd,
PO Box 269, Abingdon, Oxon
OX14 4YN
USA: Trafalgar Square Publishing,
814 N Franklin Street, Chicago,
IL 60610
USA Christian Market: Kregel
Publications, PO Box 2607, Grand
Rapids, MI 49501

THE LION BOOK OF

Prayers *for* Me

Christina Goodings

Illustrated by Emily Bolam

LI🐾N
CHILDREN'S

Contents

5012732

242.8
Go

Dear God, this is me

God, look down from heaven:
Here on earth you'll see
Someone looking upwards –
That someone is me.

I get up

I wake
I wash
I dress
I say:
Thank you
God
for this
new day.

I pray for the person I see in the mirror,
who's really a lot like me;
who needs to grow older and wiser and
    kinder
to be the best they can be.

I set out

Here I am
in the great big world
with everywhere to explore;
and God made me
to live as his child
and love him for evermore.

I will choose the narrow path,
I will walk the straight,
Through the wide and winding world
Up to heaven's gate.

SOPHIE PIPER

I do my best

I am only me, but I'm still someone.
I cannot do everything, but I can do
  something.
Just because I cannot do everything does
  not give me the right to do nothing.

AMISH MOTTO

We can do no great things,
Only small things with great love.

BLESSED TERESA OF CALCUTTA (1910–97)

Thank you for my family and friends

Dear God, bless all my family,
as I tell you each name;
and please bless each one differently
for no one's quite the same.

May I be a good friend

We
not me.

Share
not tear.

Mend
not end

and so
befriend.

Sophie Piper

Little deeds of kindness,
Little words of love,
Help to make earth happy,
Like the heaven above.

Julia Carney (1823–1908)

May love surround us

The circle of my family and
the circle of my friends
are safe within the circle
of the love that never ends.

SOPHIE PIPER

Bless those who help us

Thank you, dear God,
for the many kind people
who help us along our way,
who smile when we're happy,
who care when we're tearful,
who keep us safe all through the day.

Thank you for all I have

For blessings here
and those in store
we give thanks now
and evermore.

My food

Let us say
A thank you prayer
For the food
That's here to share.

Harvest of leaf,
Harvest of fruit,
Harvest of stem,
Harvest of root;
Harvest of lowland,
Harvest of hill,
Harvest that all
May eat their fill.

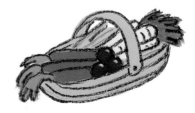

My home

Thank you for the roof above,
thank you for the floor,
thank you for the windowpanes,
thank you for the door.

Thank you that I have a home –
a place to be inside,
a place to share with those I love,
the door held open wide.

So many things

We give thanks
for all the things that are our very own.

We give thanks
for all the things that are ours to share.

We give thanks
for all the things that others share with us.

We give thanks
for all the things we can enjoy together.

Thank you for all I can do

Thank you for the things we love.
Are you watching from above?
As we play and draw and sing,
do you wish you could join in?

VICTORIA TEBBS

For the out-and-about days

Out and about
And feeling small
God, please help me
If I fall.

Out and about
And walking tall
Trusting God
Not scared at all.

34

For my birthday

All around the seasons
another year has flown.
Now it is my birthday
and look how I have grown
all around the seasons
to celebrate this day
with everyone who loves me
and God to guide my way.

For holidays

Father, lead us through this day
As we travel on our way.
Be our safety, be our friend,
Bring us to our journey's end.

I love to have sand between my toes,
to watch the tide as it comes and goes,
to pick up shells and throw them away:
thank you, dear God, for my holiday.

For Christmas

I count the days to Christmas
and I watch the evening sky.
I want to see the angels
as to Bethlehem they fly.

I'm watching for the wise men
and the royal shining star.
Please may I travel with them?
Is the stable very far?

I count the days to Christmas
as we shop and bake and clean.
The lights and tinsel sparkle,
and yet deep inside I dream

that as we tell the story
of Lord Jesus and his birth,
the things of everyday will fade
as heaven comes to earth.

For Easter

Winter is grey
but Easter is green:
all through the world
God's blessings are seen.

Winter is silver,
Easter is gold:
all through the world
God's love must be told.

Thank you for the world

Thank you, dear God,

For the good earth:
I stand upon it.

For the clean air:
I can breathe it.

For the pure water:
I can drink it.

For the fiery sun:
It warms the good earth.

For animals

All things bright and beautiful,
All creatures great and small,
All things wise and wonderful,
The Lord God made them all.

Mrs C. F. Alexander (1818–95)

Baby creatures, just awakened,
You are part of God's creation;
Baby creatures, oh, so small,
God is father of us all.

For little creatures

The little bugs that scurry,
The little beasts that creep
Among the grasses and the weeds
And where the leaves are deep:
All of them were made by God
As part of God's design.
Remember that the world is theirs,
Not only yours and mine.

For wild things

Thank you, dear God, for the wild birds
and their wild and noisy cry;

for the wild hills and the wild woods
where the wild wind whistles by;

for the wild weeds with their wild seeds
that wind all the earth around;

for in this wide world of wildness
such wonderful beauty is found.

Please look after me

The sky is so big
and I am so small:
never forget me, God,
never at all.

Help me to say sorry

Dear God,
For the little things I have done wrong,
I am sorry.

For the big things I have done wrong,
I am sorry.

For the things I didn't even know were
   wrong,
I am sorry.

For all things I need to put right,
Make me strong.

<small>SOPHIE PIPER</small>

Dear God,
Help me to forget my mistakes but to
remember what they taught me.

Be near when I am sad

O God,
be to me
like the evergreen tree
and shelter me in your shade,
and bless me again
like the warm gentle rain
that gives life to all you have made.

Dear God,
Please be my special friend;
closer than a hug,
softer than a quilt,
braver – far braver –
than even my best-loved bear.

Be my good shepherd

Dear God, you are my shepherd,
You give me all I need,
You take me where the grass grows green
And I can safely feed.

You take me where the water
Is quiet and cool and clear;
And there I rest and know I'm safe
For you are always near.

BASED ON PSALM 23

Keep me safe this night

Lord, keep us safe this night,
Secure from all our fears;
May angels guard us while we sleep,
Till morning light appears.

JOHN LELAND (1754–1841)

Bless us all

God bless all those that I love;
God bless all those that love me;
God bless all those that love those that I love,
And all those that love those that love me.

TRADITIONAL

The moon shines bright,
The stars give light
Before the break of day;
God bless you all
Both great and small
And send a joyful day.

TRADITIONAL

In the words that Jesus taught

Our Father in heaven,
hallowed be your name,
your kingdom come,
your will be done,
on earth as in heaven.
Give us today our daily bread.
Forgive us our sins
as we forgive those who sin against us.
Lead us not into temptation
but deliver us from evil.

THE LORD'S PRAYER

For the kingdom, the power,
and the glory are yours
now and for ever.
Adam

A TRADITIONAL ENDING FOR THE PRAYER

Index of first lines

3/13

DATE DUE
